N

IRON-ON CONSTELLATIONS
EMILY POHL-WEARY

TIGHTROPE BOOKS
Toronto • Detroit

CONTENTS

WHAT I LEARNED GROWING UP IN PARKDALE
For S.B.

Cars never stop for pedestrians
Kids should buy cigarettes in ones, it's cheaper
Lake Ontario was once clean enough to swim in
Cadillacs invariably carry pimps
You can't find parking on Sundays
Never trust others
Pick your nose when a pusher approaches
If you steal, you'll get beat to a pulp
The cops only make you bleed worse
Guardian Angels are worse than cops
Hookers earn a decent living
The pimp always gets tired
Old women live alone
Boys trick you into giving them blow jobs
Residents' associations hassle single women
The guy who owns the grocery store kicks his workers
My babysitter turns tricks
After dark, every car carries one man
Hide-and-seek is a dangerous game
People can survive anything

BEST VIOLIN

With the very best violin
strapped to the back of his dad's grey trench coat,
he survived somehow, wrote bad poetry,
rode that rotting skateboard like
a blocked beat poet in search of inspiration.

The class belle loved his scent of pallid suicide.
Skipping class, palms sweaty.
He was chubby acid-washed jeans.
She was laughing blue eyeshadow,
smudged mascara, black-cat earrings.

They were Betty and Archie,
playing strings on Wednesdays,
skating in Kensington Market.
A year of punks against skinheads,
Spadina buses, escalators,
peanut butter cups and vintage clothing shops.

He wrote "love" in her yearbook,
so she introduced him to her mother.
They talked on the phone for hours.
And, though she faked it,
she couldn't play the violin to save her life.

FIFTEEN

Water for a tourist,
an overdeveloped sun
in a photograph with a lake.

So happy to swim in foam
cool and smooth,
like the beer that pulls him under.

He dreams while he sinks
of the cigarettes kept dry
for the other side.

Liquid fills his lungs slowly.
The cellphone hippies on the next hill
keep drumming, dancing in the hot sun.

I listen as their drums
drown all other sounds of
laughter, crying.

There's a shiny body bag by the side of the water.
Screaming blue hair sits in the sand,
rocking, watching the rescue team drag.

Back in the city:
pavement flows like a grey lake,
life flows into another fifteen-year-old body.

GIFT FROM THE EIGHTIES

After Frida Kahlo's painting Unos cuantos Piquetitos

Because the car might fill with CO_2,
they would read the Sunday morning paper slowly,
then wrap each other up, like gifts to be opened later.
Fifty-two layers of cartoons and tape.

Once, on a Tuesday,
playing fifty-two pick-up (she was the loser)
blood gushed onto the carpet.
Scattered like cards.

The clang of an alarm clock.
She cannot be whole, his voice echoed.
Hole is what he called her,
after she ran away to zero.

"Just a few small nips," he laughed later,
shaking his head into the foaming beer.

DISTORTED BARBIE DOLL

They find her hinges, bend them back,
twist the joints around, watch her facial features blur
detach spin glue.

Oops, her head's on wrong.

Bruised inside and out,
she is a big flopping doll with no owner,
a study of desire to fit into the crowd.

Just for the massive fun of it all
We party! We watch TV!
while the sweet giant
has her kneecaps bashed in.

Finally she has become girl-size
(and lies).

THROAT FLOWER

Today, walking,
we talk as a flower sprouts deep in my throat.
Spewing green, red petals push out.
I submit to growth.

      wishing it would

Wind bends stems, riffles leaves,
thick stalk forces my teeth open.
Walking, walking.

"Could be worse," you muse.
"A thorn bush or prickly evergreen."

I'd spit pine needles at you.

"Don't try to fight it,
perhaps you swallowed a seed."

Disturbed. Tickles my nostrils
when you kiss me.

I gnash at the green stalk,
tastes like wooden asparagus.

go away

ROCKET GIRL

Day breaks like a lightning flash,
no gradual sunrise for her.

She is the adrenaline flush of a girl in love;
a neuron firing, a steroid injecting.

She moves too fast for nature,
missed this morning's passage from night into day.

She is a sound bite of personality,
in disguise as a full human being.

THE HOSPITAL

Tempting, tantalizing, repulsing
your knowledge, or lack thereof,
is hung like a worm on a sterile hook,
promising deliverance and health.

If only I don't mind to wait wait wait wait wait.

I smell like vomit, chemicals, starch-stiff gowns.
You wear perfume or cologne.

Like God or my father peering down at me:
radiation baby's very sick.

One thing's for certain in the fluorescent hotel:
You prick, I bleed.

DOCTOR OF MINE

Come speak to me professionally.
I know it's your job.

Your smile is charming,
it keeps me distracted.
After you leave, I scream, "Take me."
Take my blood.

It's not personal.
I fall in love with movie stars.
Everyone loves a hero for a week.
Years later, I'll laugh at the curve of an eyebrow,
the way you did that exam in semi-darkness.

Today, I soften reality.
Sure you can feel my abdomen,
I stay sane this way.

Tomorrow, you will become
a blond memory of hospital,
confusion, and pain.

Ramblings from a heart
that somehow, amazingly,
pumps me through today.

SEMI-PRIVATE

Her skin is shriveled,
not peaches and cream,
hair obviously not the colour God gave her.

She eats Jell-O,
stains her lips orange.
Pas ben bon, pas cinq étoiles.

But then again, we're in the hospital,
it's not a five-star hotel.

See the darkened spots on her skin?
They are battle scars:
five children, only two daughters,
and they were no help.
The sons, well, you know about sons.
They visit in between their jobs,
their lives, their busyness.

But me, I'm all alone,
so young: *une étudiante.*

She hopes it's not serious.

YAWN

Another great big evening,
watching the lovely weather outside my window,
sharing the view with four other beds and company.

Êtes-vous froid?
Mais non, l'air frais est si beau.

C'est un beau printemps, n'est ce pas?
Oui, pour ceux qui peuvent l'apprécier :
être dehors c'est un luxe.

Please,
you'll just get gloom in the glow of the sunset.
I rarely feel like talking these days.
My head keeps me company, though not comfort.

A yawning gap in my future.

EXCISION

I would hold my stomach up
before a firing squad
with my own bare hands
if I could just remove it from me.

Replace it with a newer, healthier version.

It is beyond my control,
un-detachable,
not persuaded by reason, need, or patience.

It has a life of its own.
I don't want it hanging around anymore.

HOPE SPRINGS

There cannot be life
I must remind myself
a dozen times a day.

It's hard to think positive
in a starched-sheet bed.

The nurse wears gloves
when she touches me.

STREET TOUCH

Not one of those grey days
when the wind's touch could blow me over
when I choose the path of least resistance
just to make it home.

Today is more of a warm-wind-on-the-skin day.
I could walk forever,
wet air and your soft lips,
warm skin on my clean sheets.

Painful somehow
to allow grey wind to touch me
on the streets, not in the bedroom.
You are sex to me.

I need your strength.
You are my craving
when this warm wind stops
blowing my coat open.

BREAK THE ICE

Break me.
Break my ice.
It's been a long time coming.
It's a relief.

I sleep now,
my world has stopped spinning,
motion sickness forever.

You are life.
You are not life,
you're just a boyfriend.
A little boy kneeling before my pain.

I had a pain in my gut
like you would never believe.
If I let it, it would have torn me in half:
one leg, one arm on each side.

Useless.

I AM A SHOOTING STAR

I am a shooting star
watch my glittering tail.

It stretches behind me
as I rush past your window.

You might as well wave hello.

Pain bounces off.
My perspective is change.

You could try to catch me in your butterfly net.
I would simply burn a hole in the webbing.

My tail is meant to light up the sky.
Watch me fly.

BECAUSE

You never cross at the crosswalk in the summer,
but I don't care.
The stoplight glints off the tracks
like the porch light in the cat's eyes.
The neighbour wears bruises to the grocery.
We meet sometimes, near the broccoli.

VIRUS

The first thing I did
was paint all over your photo.
Erase with pink strokes
so no one will know
you were in my computer.

CAST-OFFS

In the winter she eats my pickings:
stale bread and seeds.
Survives throughout it all:
ice, storms, freezing.
She could fly away at any time
on pale brown wings, but doesn't.

BACKHOE

I am in love with the backhoe loader
who clears my snow when it gets really bad.

My grey-steel, yellow-painted backhoe loader
leaps into action like a muscle,
like a flesh-eating dinosaur.

Last night we kissed
beneath the moonlit snowbanks,
cold steel jaws against hot lips,
frozen together, the flakes fell down around us.

I felt his strength,
touched every inch of his frame.

Today I stand in his white world,
watch him work.
Lifting, pushing, crushing the ice,
sweeping aside a drift of snow
with the same caress he uses to touch me.

THE WOODEN

Now I remember
(unwanted, perhaps)
a fruit stand opening
is my heart on a cold day.

The warmth of a frozen city.
The market, open for business,
comes alive like a waking dog
stretching, licking its jowls.

You are my boxes of fruit
(coaxing, perhaps).
I am the wooden fruit stand.

SUBWAY OF LOVE

I'm riding to your place patiently
when images of you seductive
are replaced by fellow passengers.

Food for fluorescent thoughts.
My brain overflowing,
I see your face superimposed on their bodies.

I'm riding the molten metal flow
you would probably call desire.

With each grinding to a halt,
my eyes devour new entrants.

We jiggle down the tracks together
for a while. I'm so sad to see them go.

The doors' ka-chunk
release me again and again.
Ding-dong go the wedding bells,
warning me.

Enter Exit Enter Exit Enter:
sixteen stops of in and out.

After, I wander up the stairs
through the muggy stars to you, waiting smooth,
reading my eyes like that stupid book.

JOHN DOE IS MY ROOMMATE

I eat vegetarian pasta,
he opens Beefaroni.
Twelve grain versus Wonder Bread.

I sleep above his bedroom,
listen for voices.
Just the news, *Friends*, *Seinfeld* blaring.

He wears his television set like armour.
I don't own a TV.

No phone calls,
no dishes in the kitchen.
Haven't seen my roommate in days.

John Doe gets inside my head,
becomes my linoleum focus.

He coughs in the rushing traffic,
pisses in the rustling leaves.

Creeping past his door,
I sniff the air for decay,
press my ear to his door.
Silence.

He must be dead or dying.

SHOOTING THE SHIT
For Emily #2

My finger picks at paint.

We are sitting on old rockers out on the porch,
remembering decades of processed food:

>   rainbow tie-dye of hippies
>   who drum badly
>
>   movies with idols
>   we wanted to dance like
>
>   spin-the-bottle kissing games
>   going too far

The summer sun,
scraped knees and stained glass,
anarchist patches, babies, mosquitoes, abortions.

We live close, like the hairs on my leg.

My finger peels off chips of your life
while the sun peeks in
through slats in my clothing.

I am wind.
I am holes.
I am gaps.

TO BUILD A HOME

Start with a firm foundation.
Place the bricks just so.
Avoid regrets, ghosts, fist fights, unemployment,
dead cats buried in the garden, low self-esteem,
petty thievery, bullying, and assisted suicide.
Cement should slide in between the scandals,
forming bonds and hardening in the hot sun.
A roof must bridge the walls.
A swing set placed beneath the lilacs.
Mousetraps purchased, installed.
Finally, despite initial resistance,
erect a high fence around the entirety.

MIRROR ON QUEEN

You look at me silver.
You are just walking past.

I am the mirror in a store on Queen Street,
reflecting nothing.

You are a face,
passing by at the wrong angle.

I have seen pretty girls in tight skirts,
boys with slicked-back hair,
drunks falling into fast cars.

Words of wisdom:
"A mirror behind a glass wall should not throw stones."
Silver blankness is not a balanced state.

BRIGHTNESS

Lamp resting on my bedside table
bounces light at my aged paperback.

Colour spectrum arcs the sky,
CN Tower cuts it.

Later, the night outside my window
swallows the brightness.

Your lips and ass reflect a glare
so strong, so hot, it hurts my eyes.

LULLABY

The city lulls me to sleep:
lights and sirens and laundry.

Rhythmic rubber tires cross streetcar tracks,
an intravenous needle rips out, his heart screams,
blood spurts, a fetus aborts, a scavenger cowers,
concrete buildings throw shadows.

Only eight inches of hot, hard flesh
and candy-floss lips will do.

MY GOLD HAIR IS SO UNRELIABLE

Green light
the city rips past.
Rain in Chinatown, fish markets,
garbage bags oozing brown urine.

Saturday night in dance-club heaven,
teenage girls crumble under speeding tires
lost in the midnight of boy love,
caught in flashes of light.

I sparkle brightly
until hard night wind attacks my miniskirt,
high heels burn fire,
fueled by wandering.

I always return
to your smooth beer drinking,
bubbles of love.

The taxicab driver tries,
but he cannot bring me home fast enough.

Your eyes in the window.
I walk up the path,
my left shoe grazes the curb—fucking toes.

It might have come from the neighbours,
"I guess I don't love you"
rippled out in all directions.

SEPARATION/STARS

Her name is Emily too,
but she is just a tired fairy
with a knack for loneliness,
stars glued down to decorate her T-shirt,
match her eyes.

She will wait on my table,
offer me tea filled with sparkle dust,
shining like the liquid tears
of a fairy who danced until 3 AM
then cried late at night.
Fairy prince did not come home

So mad, she pulled her hair,
stomped, yelled, grabbed the night stars,
sewed them onto the front of that baby T.

Now all the world's stars
are iron-on constellations,
sticky playthings peeling off small breasts.

She waits
searching in the world music, the lattes, the smoothies,
for clues to bliss and the prince who never returned.

BLUEFIELDS NIGHT

Twinkle stars.
Reach up, grab a handful of familiar
to keep in her lint-dust pocket.

Home in this distant land,
they are night sky.

He is wet, hot thick air,
a hairy leg against her knobby knees.

Smell sea: open, endless depths.

Poverty wrapped in a blanket of darkness,
homeless children sleep close too,
while she sits safe in his lap.
Warm water, skin, salt, her.

She holds him,
day pain disappearing.
He watches the boats come home.

He found she here.
They are swirling in black waters

He is a star bursting out of her pocket,
lands in cupped hands,
fills a laundry basket with bright
to light the night sky.

FOREST

I see you through the forest:
misty green leaves against the grey sky.
Stifling. Humidity makes my neck damp, my face itch.

I watch you from the mountain.
You are far away, working,
turn your back, too busy to notice me staring.

I reach for binoculars to spy even better.
You disappear in an airplane.

Now you're only a reflection behind my houseplant.
Your face is in my mirror.
I waved goodbye. Did you notice?

There was a time
when we fucked happily
and I woke up secure.

MELANCHOLY

Yellow is
my presence is
slicing the rye bread of your mind thickly.

We talk in circles
over pale yellow grain,
spreading pale yellow fat,
so smooth.

Butter pushes up onto my front teeth.
I bite down hard.

Oh, I love bread and butter,
am guaranteed to eat from the soft middle out to the crust.

But you,
lost in your mazes,
you barely even noticed me.

Me.
I could have been your knife forever.

ENEMY

Out flows grey matter
through cracks in his head.

Her stomach is a landscape.
His finger picks at the scars
under the sunny window of her bedroom.

He is searching for that perfect blend
of disregard and beauty.

She is hoping for a life.

Food not bombs is their synonym
for out on the streets.

BALLS

The lanes are neon,
my shoes are black and white.

I eat your french fries
with loads of red ketchup,
watch rolling hard balls everywhere,
picture your head.

I hate bowling
but smile anyway at your pals.

Her hair is the dark blond of my underarms,
the difference is that you have known me longer.

COFFEE BREAK

Marvin horks on the sidewalk
like it's his living-room floor—
a dark glob slops on the pavement.

>   *I want to call you*
>   *when we pass a phone booth.*

Marvin and me,
we sip coffee anyway.
I drink it black, unsweetened,
fumbling with the phone book in my hip pocket.

>   *Never could*
>   *pick up the phone:*
>   *white cord, white receiver.*

These tables are pretentious.
This coffee tastes like rubber.

You—naked in my kitchen,
my Bodum of black coffee.

The way you add sugar and cream
makes me see stars.

YOU FOG ME OUT

The day starts early.
I want to be awake
when thunder cracks the hungry clouds.

My kettle screams,
your mind is an ocean.

Before the sun,
my face in the bathroom mirror is electric
until the hot and wet of your coffee breath fogs me out.

I offer to make toast with cheese.
You cannot eat to save your life.

We smoke chocolate cigarettes instead,
laugh about people we know:
friends, family, enemies.

You offer to buy breakfast
before the marathon to making my life a picture book.

For once, I just don't know what to say.

PICKING AT WALLS AND ARMIES

Despite the fact we are all paper cut-out dolls,
if I could paint (like the great Dali or Matisse or Kahlo)
I would portray my lover in blacks and reds,
infuse him with the correct dosage of passion, mystery, and pain.

Eyes open through stone riot days,
we can always wear steel-toed boots under the sheets,
explode together like paint bombs,
whittle away our time, picking at walls and armies.

We may be the future
with trendy purple haircuts,
but when he sleeps like death or illness
there is so little I can do.

CHICAGO

The sun streaks.
We giggle over tea,
kiss wet in that lick-my-cunt way.
The kind of guy I've always wanted
tastes like a goth girl.

We love the anarchists,
street workers, carpenters, gravediggers.
Walk for miles through ugly American streets,
joke about their fat food and barbed wire.

The art museum makes us argue:
cubism and false politics.
I want to eat the vegetables in the garden,
but you would just die.

On the way home,
strangers' underwear yells at us.
Your hair is wild,
driven to the point of corn fields
whipping past the train.

SPECIAL COLLECTION
For B.M.

Some of the Group of Seven
are known for their bravery and passion.

Despite ourselves,
we are moved by the gouache, acrylic, oils
tempera sunset in the bush,
dappled thicket, wildflowers, twisted maple.

How scandalous to paint nothing but trees!
How primitive!
How Canada!

When there are people,
the subjects are always women,
the painter's bearded gaze and puffing stogie
always implied.

Is this Canada?
These conquistadores; staunch rip-off artists
surrounded by second growth, green regret,
and early death.

THE SENSATIONALIST

She is dyeing her hair with a bottle:
red, yellow, orange from the five-and-dime.
Watching those green earrings turn gold.

All dreams were shattered when he left.

There's no money
in the life of a cliché princess
who gets fucked once a day
by the Prozac™ of loneliness.

Glamour rejects her discount jewellery
and love: a series of chipped teeth
swept under the rug.

ARTIST

A tree on the street to the bar
was yellow, lush, and weeping.

After the eleven o'clock news
a tree is a lovely thing.

When we met
it was either tears or love.
But you are an artist and
we are all in love with artists.

A cigarette,
rum from your purse,
you made love to him.

When you looked away
the wind in your eyes screamed:
"My past precedes me."

I left the bar
because it was raining.

IT'S ALL FRIDA K'S FAULT

For never plucking that big black eyebrow
For surviving despite the pain
For painting herself until her last breath
For looking inward at inspiration
Being ashamed
Painting her lips red
Her blood red
Her fetus
Her ugly
For allowing herself to have wretched days
Cross-dressing at age 19, Mexico, 1926
Crying in public
For loving flowers
For shocking
For the beauty she saw in the mirror
For being sensual when she couldn't move by herself

CREDITS

Several poems were originally published in the (maga)zines *Kiss Machine*, *Throat Flower,* and *They're Just Words*. "My Gold Hair is So Unreliable," "Distorted Barbie Doll," and "Subway of Love" were published in *Fireweed*. "What I Learned Growing Up in Parkdale" was in *Taddle Creek* and *Fish Piss*. "Best Violin" was in *Taddle Creek*. "It's All Frida K's Fault" was in *Dig*. "John Doe is My Roommate," "Separation/Stars," and "Because" appeared in *The Writing Space Journal*.

ACKNOWLEDGEMENTS

As always, hugs for the big family and kisses for Jesse Hirsh. Thanks to Halli Villegas and Keith Daniel at Tightrope Books; Willow Dawson, cover artist extraordinaire; and Conan Tobias, world's best copy editor. Early versions of many of these poems were picked apart by members of the Hoity-Toity Writers' Group: Jim Munroe, Jeff Chapman, Paul Hong, Paola Poletto, Ryan Bigge, and Jessica Westhead. Lisa Rundle, Julia Pohl-Miranda, and Hal Niedzviecki also read drafts of the manuscript.

ABOUT THE AUTHOR

Emily Pohl-Weary's first novel, *A Girl Like Sugar*, about a girl who's haunted by her dead rock star boyfriend, was published in 2004. The *Globe and Mail* called it "wonderfully explicit" and "quietly redemptive."

Earlier that year, she toured across North America with her critically acclaimed anthology, *Girls Who Bite Back: Witches, Mutants, Slayers and Freaks*. In 2002, she co-authored *Better to Have Loved: The Life of Judith Merril*, a biography of her grandmother's life, which won a Hugo Award and was a finalist for the Toronto Book Award.

Since 2000, she has edited *Kiss Machine* magazine, a conga line of culture. She's currently writing a four-part series of comics, *Violet Miranda: Girl Pirate*, with artist Willow Dawson, about two girls who find adventure on the high seas. Her young adult mystery novel, the first of a series, is forthcoming from Annick Press in 2006.

Visit her website at http://emily.openflows.org